Sheds

"I Shed, Therefore I Am."

By
J. V. Houlihan, Jr.

"If a man wants to stay married, he'd better have a shed."
Anonymous

www.celticlegendbooks.com
Copyright©2013 by J. V. Houlihan, Jr.
svcelticlegend@hotmail.com
Art: Diane Gay
Cover Design: J.V. Houlihan, Jr.
Technical Consultant: Pat Bowlby

Dedicated
To all people who have fearlessly chosen their true path

Special Thanks

To

Christopher Walken

For

My father, who possessed a Yankee sensibility and an Irish heartbeat

Introduction

Nota Bene: *This book is not necessarily about what the reader may interpret as a traditional meaning of the word shed. The word is used metaphorically. In fact, the author admits that he once tried to build a shed, and failed. It was not plumb, nor square. Quite frankly, it was a terrible eyesore and it leaked. However, the author must also mention that at least he made the attempt to build one.*

According to Webster's Dictionary:

Main entry: **Shed**
Function: *noun*
Etymology: alteration of earlier *shadde*, probably from Middle English *shade*.
Date: 1557

1 a: a slight structure built for shelter or storage; especially: a single-storied building with one or more sides enclosed.

2. *Archaic*: **Hut**

The author does not want to bother the reader with the verb usage of the word shed.

Table of Contents

Birth of "Shed" Metaphor	1
Sheds	3
Edith Wharton	7
Norman Rockwell	11
Herman Melville	14
Mark Twain	18
Arthur Miller	25
<u>Contemporaries</u>	
Tim Philbrick	33
Mark Holden	42
Cameron Greenlee	51
Jane Musky	59
Diane Gay	67
Cindy McDonald-Houlihan	73

Birth of the *Shed* Metaphor

A few years ago, I reconnected with an old friend, Tim, from my wild scuffling days as a saloon singer. I remember talking with this guy, thirty years ago, about who our heroes were. I'd been writing songs since I was a kid, and had the same heroes as many young guitar picking kids of the sixties, such as Bob Dylan, Gordon Lightfoot et al. My friend had different kinds of heroes such as Newporter John Goddard, a designer of furniture from the 1750s. Also, an old Yankee, John Northup, was his mentor and friend. Tim's a furniture maker of the highest order. I'll talk more about this later.

One night during dinner in Newport, Rhode Island, I told Tim I wanted to show him my sailboat, where I do my writing in the winter time. It was near the restaurant. I'd graduated from writing songs to attempting more complex manuscripts. "It's kind of a hideout," I said, "my own little place to tinker with words." Tim said he heard a guy once say, "If a man wants to stay married, he'd better have a shed." I readily agreed with him as I ate my steak, and my writing wheels began turning. After dinner, we walked over to the docks near Bowen's Wharf, and I proudly showed off my sailboat, as most boat guys normally do. After I dropped Tim off in Narragansett,

Rhode Island, I went home and wrote seven hundred words about my idea of what a shed is. The piece flew out of me, which is usually a good sign, as I like it when writing comes to me quickly. The next morning, I pitched it to the editor of the *Block Island Times*, and it appeared in the paper in that week's edition.

While working at my job as a dock worker at the Block Island Ferry Company in Point Judith, I got lots of feedback as a result of the article. A friend of mine, an artist, suggested that I write a book about the sheds of various people. So here it is. As you read the opening piece entitled, *Sheds*, I want you to ask yourself a very simple question. I want you to ask yourself what or where your shed is. You will note my thesis (if I sound academic, sorry, it's the former school teacher coming out of me) may sound inferred to some, and directly stated to others. Nevertheless, be mindful of the responsibility of the question, since there will be an assignment at the end of this book (sorry, the teacher thing again). The most fun part of writing this book was having complete autonomy in choosing the people whose *Sheds* I wanted to explore and discuss. At this time in my life, it is all about having autonomy, as I'm sure all of the baby-boomers reading this book will agree. Finally, I also feel very strongly, that in this fast-paced, fragmented, digitalized, media driven, thirty-second spot, advertisement driven attention span, and heavily information overloaded (please stop me!!!) age in which we live, perhaps it would be good for all of us to stop and smell the roses, on the way to our *Shed*.

Sheds

"If a man wants to stay married, he better have a *Shed*." Forget political correctness for a moment. A *Shed* is simply a metaphor for individuation, a place where a guy goes to stay connected to himself. I can only talk about guy *Sheds*—because I'm a guy. I'm not one of those handy guys who build things in the basement—which is a *Shed*. My brother does, and he makes cool stuff. I'm not into the train set or the ship in the bottle thing. I pick up a hammer, and my kids laugh at me when I whack my thumb. The most tactile thing I ever did was play the guitar, which has shed-ness, but to me it's not really a *Shed*.

A wise woman will let her man go to his *Shed* and enjoy his absence. My wife enjoys the silence. My belief is that when a guy goes to his *Shed*, he comes back a better guy. Moreover, when a guy goes to his *Shed*, his wife can go to hers too. It's a win-win deal.

The real issue here is whether people know where, or more importantly, what their *Shed* is. I just turned on my laptop today, and these are the first sentences typed on this new tool of mine, in my *Shed*. A really bright computer guy I know got this thing for me for short money. It has no Internet stuff: music, videos, etc. Simplicity is all I want; I simply want to write sentences. Period. I'm a Luddite. I've thrown sand, rocks and glue into the gears of the computerization of teaching. I was an English teacher, who went kicking, screaming, and raging into the computer age. I wrote out my tests in long hand and watched administrators cringe, and I loved it. I'd hold up tattered copies of books and say, "These still work!" Now here I am writing on this laptop in my Shed; oh the irony of it all.

My *Shed* is 30 feet long, weighs 9,000 pounds, and has a ten and a half foot beam. It floats in a slip in a marina, in Newport Harbor, Rhode Island. My shed serves many purposes. My wife, dog and I sail her in the spring, summer and fall; we have fun on the boat. I also stay aboard her some nights in the summer for work-related reasons—I work for the Block Island Ferry—and it's easier to stay in the harbor, rather than go home to Point Judith, since we run one of our ferries out of Newport. In winter though, the boat becomes my Shed, and it is where I make what I like to make most—sentences, like the ones you're reading right now.

I have several tools in my *Shed* besides this laptop. In the main cabin, I keep my other tools within easy reach. When I need to craft short, punchy sentences, I pull down Hemingway for ideas. A torn, battered and over-read copy of McMurtry's *Lonesome Dove* may inspire dialogue. Twain's *Huckleberry Finn* sits next to McMurtry. If tone is required, then I pull out Pete Hamill's *Forever* or *Downtown*. If honing metaphors is required, I grab the best tool I have, which is the Robert Fagles' translation of Homer's *Odyssey*. If my voice is required to sound professorial, yet down to earth, Nat Philbrick comes off the shelf. When I start to take making sentences too seriously, I grab *Curb Your Enthusiasm, The Book*, or anything by Carl Hiaasen.

All of my tools have been used over and over again, and I have become familiar with their feel. Some recent tools added to my collection are Cormac McCarthy's, *No Country for Old Men*, and *The Road*. Sometimes I lend my tools to other sentence makers. Recently, I gave away a tool that was hard for me to use, but may be of use to this other craftsman I know—*Underworld*, by Don Delillo. It was a hard and complex tool to handle—like a dangerous power tool.

When I'm done writing my sentences, and they've become essays, short stories or vignettes, there is one other tool I need to use. I take *The Writer's Market* off the shelf, and look for a place to publish my finished work. Then I leave my *Shed*, go home, tell my wife what I made, and show it to her. She says, "That's nice dear," and then we go walk our dog.

Edith Wharton

As I stated earlier, I can only speak about guy *Sheds* because I'm a guy; however, I can appreciate a woman's *Shed*. I'll never claim to understand women, but I honor and respect their *Sheds*. Recently, my wife and I were in the Berkshires at a cousin's wedding, and she suggested that we go to Edith Wharton's home in Lenox, Massachusetts, called The Mount. She had visited Emily Dickinson's home, last fall, and thought it was a great place. Furthermore, Wharton is a favorite author of hers; so off we went.

Edith Wharton was a prolific writer, who was very much her own woman. "There was in me one secret retreat where I wished no one to intrude." I'll say that Edith knew what her *Shed*, was. At a young age, she'd ensconce herself in her father's library, and create her own stories. Also, she loved reading books aloud. She was born into New York society, and summered in Newport, yet she felt stifled. Her mother figured the best thing to do with her bright daughter was to marry her off. Relationships were not an easy thing for this self- assured woman. In her novel *House of Mirth,* she writes of a protagonist, who tries to escape the social clutter and pressure of

New York society; it was a shadow of her life. She was not born to follow anyone's lead.

She wrote her first novel at sixteen, and produced forty books over a span of forty years. Although she wrote in different parts of New England, Europe, and the U.K., The Mount was where she loved to write the most. In fact, she had the house built specifically for writing. This place also became a meeting place for friends and writers. Henry James became a close friend of hers, and would visit her at The Mount. Edith designed this elegant yet simple house, which she considered her "first real home." We toured the unpretentious rooms, and I was taken by the austerity and functionality of their design.

Edith wrote in her bedroom, and dropped the pages to the floor. I love this image of Edith comfortable in her *Shed*, inking off great prose, and casually dropping the pages to the floor. Her secretary would then collect them for typing. The view of her gardens was an extension of her *Shed*, and looked like they had the stamp of Olmstead on them. My wife informed me that Edith designed them with her niece, Beatrix Farrand, who was a renowned landscape architect. Edith told her friends that she was a better landscape gardener than a novelist. Her self-deprecation was also very attractive to me.

She and her friends would drive around the Berkshires and observe the countryside in her motor car. Then Edith would retreat to her bedroom, undisturbed, and write. *Ethan Frome* was a result of these outings. I want to revisit *Ethan Frome* now; I haven't read the novel since high school. (See what happens when you take a look at where people do what they do?) Edith Wharton was a woman who believed that "Books have souls," and I agree. Edith was a woman who truly knew the value of a *Shed*, and she had a beauty in the Berkshires.

Edith Wharton's value system was crystallized while touring battle fields during World War II. She was a humanitarian, and a fearless writer. She examined her values, and rather than taking the path of a lifetime of comfort and social station, she chose to take the path of an introspective, vibrant writer. She once told a reporter that she spoke through her writing, and that what kind of toothpaste she preferred, or what the perks of a cold bath were, was of no interest to anyone. In other words, in the grand scheme of things, stuff like this didn't matter. Today, in our celebrity obsessed culture, I believe Edith would have taken refuge—from the trivial pursuits of the mass media—in her *Shed* in the Berkshires. She would not be an easy interview for Barbra Walters.

Norman Rockwell

After visiting The Mount, we headed over to the Norman Rockwell Museum in Stockbridge, Massachusetts. My wife and I both love his work. In my view, Stockbridge was Rockwell's personal *Shed*. He said, "I know everyone in Stockbridge," and I bet he did. He also said, "I paint life as I would like it to be." Rockwell was an illustrator, and was very insecure about his work; he didn't consider it art.

His studio/*Shed* was originally right next to his house in the center of town, and it's there that he produced much of his work. To me, Norman Rockwell was the consummate Yankee—he had talent, ingenuity, and a savage work ethic. His original studio/*Shed*, was moved from the center of the town of Stockbridge, to the site of the museum just a few miles away.

I couldn't wait to see where this guy painted. After a tour of the museum, which contains all three hundred covers of the *Saturday Evening Post*, we walked over to the artist's *Shed*. It was set up just the way Rockwell had it when he worked there. His *Shed* was orderly and contained his library, whose authors ranged from EL Greco to Picasso. His easel and brushes were as they had been when his costumed models posed for him. Rockwell was a collector of myriad costumes, and props. His brushes looked clean and ready to use. There was a small teapot that he used sitting by a window. Also, there was a small bunk where he could take his power naps. I especially liked the small bunk he had in his *Shed*—it reminded me of the bunk in my own *Shed*.

Rockwell's work has a strong emotional pull for me still. Here was a man, who understood the human condition, and lived at a time of great change. His painting of the young black girl being escorted to school, an example of his later work, shows that the idyllic life in Stockbridge was not a metaphor for our country. He painted Richard Nixon; Rockwell knew, all was not well in this world. Maybe that's why his *Shed* was so orderly, and he painted the images he did. It was a special experience standing in his *Shed*. I had a similar respect for Edith's, as she too understood the human condition, and valued human relations. Both of these special places made a strong and unforgettable impression on my wife and me.

Herman Melville

We figured that while we were up in the hills, we may as well go to Herman Melville's *Shed*, in Arrowhead. At the tender age of twenty-two, Herman Melville signed on to the whale ship *Acushnet* for a three year voyage which began in New Bedford, Massachusetts. I'll go out on a limb here and say that this was an act of faith and a demonstration of guts for Melville. As far as I can see, there was nothing romantic about working on a whaling ship in the 1800s. All one needs to do is read Nat Philbrick's, *In the Heart of the Sea*, to get what I mean by this. I'm sure after three grueling years of this kind of work, Melville had plenty of material for a novel or three, but I'm also sure that he'd had a snootful of the whaling life as well, and was more than happy to walk on terra firma.

In 1850, Melville moved with his family to Pittsfield, Massachusetts from the bustle of New York City, so he could farm and write. Perhaps the mountains and valleys reminded him of the sea. (It is said, that he admired Mt. Graylock from his home.) Maybe the changing weather conditions affected the forest, as it did the ocean; calm one minute, chaotic and stormy the next. It was here at Arrowhead that he completed *Moby Dick*. He also wrote *The*

Confidence Man and *The Piazza Tales* there. Melville had some great writers to establish friendships with in the Berkshire Hills. He befriended Oliver Wendell Holmes and Nathaniel Hawthorne during his thirteen years at Arrowhead. He later returned to New York in 1863. I guess the quiet of the farm country was as deadening as the hustle and bustle of the city was nerve racking. (I'll leave this for the scholars to ponder.) Quite honestly, I'm really just interested in where he penned his stories.

Arrowhead was very modest compared to Edith's home. Although we could only look in the windows—the homestead was closed for the season—it appeared to be a simple, comfortable home. Melville's *Shed* was his library in his home in the hills. This is where he wrote his great American tome about a tortured soul named Captain Ahab. As we roamed around the outbuildings and main house, I imagined his *Shed* with scrimshaw, tattered copies of classic literature, manuscripts, works in progress, doodlings, side notes, ink wells, pens, pencils, coffee cups (he must've drunk coffee), and perhaps an old trunk filled with artifacts of his voyaging days; I wondered if he was an organized guy. Perhaps the stunning view of Mt. Graylock filled his vision, and inspired him to craft his sentences and hone his metaphors. Finally, I wondered if Melville wrote *Bartelby the Scrivener*, in his *Shed* here in the Berkshires. I liked teaching that story in my teaching days. Where did Bartelby, the copying clerk; the non-conformist, non-linear man come from in Melville's imagination? Maybe his days clerking in the Custom's House in New York City is where Bartelby evolved. The narrator in the story thinks that Bartelby is a "safe" man and a "conformist;"

when he is first hired his mien was placid. He was wrong. When he told Bartelby to do the mind-numbing job of a law copyist, Bartelby would simply say, "I would prefer not to." After first reading *Bartleby the Scrivener*, I could understand why Melville signed on aboard the *Acushnet*, rather than be a clerk. Maybe Melville had a shipmate who told the First Mate aboard the *Acushnet*, "I would prefer not to," when told by his superior to place stinking, rancid whale blubber into the boiling cauldron called the Try-Works—a nasty job I'm sure—and was given a dirtier job. All I can tell you is that Herman Melville was a great writer, who had most assuredly, a great *Shed*, and that I was lucky to have had a chance to peek into the window of it. I guess I'm an easily amused guy.

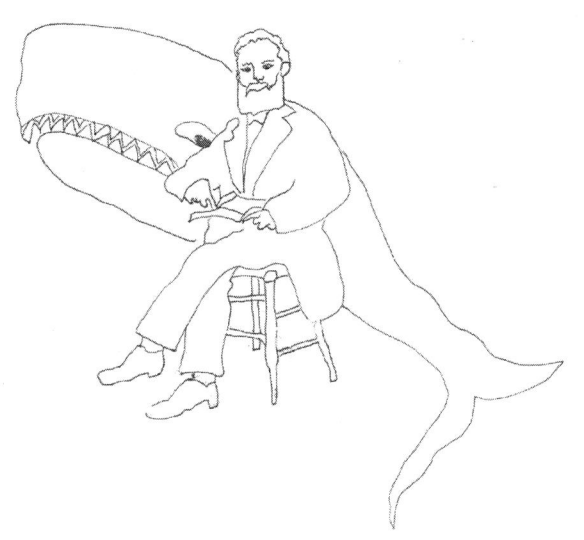

Mark Twain

The man I consider the consummate man of letters is author Mark Twain. Having taught his book *Huckleberry Finn*, and several of his shorter works, I grew to admire the man's work ethic and brains. I took a copy of a Twain biography out to my sailboat/*Shed* two summers ago, and embarked innocently on a broad study of this very complex man of letters. In Ron Power's biography *Mark Twain: A Life*, I found just reading about his life was exhausting; forget about actually being this guy Mark Twain, who possessed an incredible persona, or shall I say, his persona possessed him.

I usually have what I call a "boat book" for summer reading on my sailboat. It sounds innocent enough huh, "boat book," but it was a seven hundred page, mental hernia producing, and mind boggling study of an extremely complicated and driven human being. I admire several writers, alive and dead, but none of them can come close to Samuel Langhorne Clemens. Twain's pure tenacity, in my mind, sets him apart from all other writers. Plus, he was a really funny guy!

Over the years, while teaching *Life on the Mississippi*, I always looked forward to reading sections of the story aloud to my students;

especially the scene between Twain, the cub pilot, and Brown the captain of the riverboat. I'd read both characters with a southern accent. My students loved it when I'd read that particular dialogue. If you're intrigued presently, go read *Life on the Mississippi*, because this book isn't about teaching, it's about *Sheds*. Sorry I digressed, it was also a habit I had as a teacher.

Mark Twain traveled extensively as a young man. His mother was not really wild about his rambles, so he would placate her with many humorous letters. In Powers' biography, I read that he'd written in the vicinity of 50,000 to 100,000 letters over his life. These were not what some would call a letter today, rife with truncated English (texting stuff); I mean these were letters of the finest kind. If you read letters from soldiers during the Civil War, or even better, read Charles Frazier's *Cold Mountain*, you'll note an eloquence that we've lost as a nation. People wrote beautifully, with ornate penmanship in those days, and Mark Twain was part of that culture. So I can say safely, that he had lots of practice in developing his skills as a writer. Here is an example from Powers' *Mark Twain: A Life*. This quote gives an example, of how he humored his mother during his *Rambles*.

"My Dear Mother: you will doubtless be a little surprised, and somewhat angry when you receive this, and find me so far from home; but you must bear a little with me, for you know I was always the best boy you had, and perhaps you remember the people used to say to their children—'Now don't do like Orion and Henry Clemens, but take Sam for your guide!' Well, I was out of work in St. Louis, and didn't fancy loafing in such a dry place, where there is no pleasure to be seen without paying well for it, and so I thought I might as well go to New York. I packed up my duds and left for this village, where I arrived, all right this morning." Now how could a mom not love a kid like this!

Mark Twain was an observer of the good, bad and ugly of the country, which produced him. He was a flawed character, as we all are. He also had an ego; which was necessary to jettison him toward his future as a writer. If you got in his line of fire, and he didn't care for you, well, that was too bad for you. In *The Innocents Abroad*, he asks a deck hand of the ship the *Quaker City*, "Who is that spider-legged gorilla yonder with the sanctimonious countenance?" He was referring to the Chief Mate. Needless to say, Twain had no fondness toward this man. No folks, you didn't want to cross this guy, ever. You were best to fly under the radar (even though there was none in those days, you get my point), you were better off being invisible, lest you be eviscerated by the ever sharp implement of destruction, Mark Twain's pen.

After reading the "boat book," which took well past that fall and deep into the winter to finish, I had the urge to go see Mark Twain's home in Hartford, Connecticut. My wife and I planned a day trip easily enough; it was an easy sell. My wife loves to go to the homes of the "Dead Poets," in Concord, Massachusetts so it was off to Hartford. It's a trivial pursuit for me to try and describe Twain's home in Hartford. I can tell you that it took a long time to build, and it costs presently lots of money to maintain. There are however a couple of things to note, before I describe his *Shed*, which is really all I cared about seeing when we got inside this amazing house. I bit my tongue, and didn't blurt out to the tour guide, "Where did he write?" and embarrass my wife. I strolled and listened patiently to the tour guide talk about the fire place (yawn) and several other things, as we headed upstairs. One very interesting thing the Twain's had was a Venetian bed, which was bought on one of their trips to Italy. It was a beautifully hand carved work of art, in all actuality, very impressive. It was made from oak wood, with angels carved into the headboard. Mr. and Mrs. Twain slept with their heads at the foot of the bed so that they could admire the figures. It was very apparent that Twain's wife had lots of class, and she imbued him with some. By nature, Mark Twain was rough hewn.

Twain's family moved into Nook Farm, on the quiet artery of Farmington Avenue, in West Hartford, in 1874. The house was not yet completed. The Twain's were in over their heads. Twain liked the sophisticated neighborhood of Nook Farm. For neighbors (Hartford at that time was the wealthiest city in the U. S.), he had a U.S. Senator, a Governor, a Civil War General and a newspaper publisher. Moreover, right across his lawn lived Harriet Beecher Stowe, the author of *Uncle Tom's Cabin*. She was at the top of the literary food chain, and Twain felt I'm sure that he was in very good company. Remember I said Twain had an ego; not that there's anything wrong with that.

By 1880, Twain had hit pay dirt with the success of *The Adventures of Tom Sawyer*, and he and his wife Livy decided to really trick Nook Farm out properly. So they hired Associated Artists, which included Louis Comfort Tiffany, to do the work. As I stated earlier, my meager words can not describe this beautiful home. You'll just have to go there for a day trip. (Sorry for my digressing, again. Now let's get back to the tour of Nook Farm).

Finally, the guide brought us to the third floor of the Twain residence, which was known as the billiard room and this, was where Mark Twain wrote. This was his *Shed*, (one of them at least; he had another one at Elmira, New York; more about that later). The billiard room was where Twain wrote *Huckleberry Finn* and *Life on the Mississippi*. This was also where he knocked back some whisky with his pals; it was a guy's only place, a man-cave in today's parlance. It was off limits to all but his male friends and the cleaning staff. This was Twain's sanctuary. In the center of the billiard room/*Shed*, was a billiard table, naturally. Twain loved to play billiards. I can picture him taking a break from grinding out *Huckleberry Finn*, and smoking one of his ever-present cigars, while mumbling out dialogue between Jim and Huck. Or perhaps letting loose with some earwax melting profanity. (As writing cannot only be daunting, but very frustrating.) Twain said, "There ought to be a room in this house to swear in. It's dangerous to have to repress an emotion like that."

The ceiling of the billiard room/*Shed*, has billiard cues and balls inlaid into the wood. From this, I gather that Twain really liked playing billiards. (Actually, I think our tour guide said, "Twain really loved playing billiards!") As I looked to the left in this room, there was a desk near the window. On each side of the desk were two Tiffany lamps. This little writing space was what I was looking forward to, since reading Powers' biography. Next to the desk were shelves stacked with books (all the originals are tucked away safely in a vault). This is where Mark Twain penned, to me, his greatest work.

Mark Twain, the well, world traveled man of letters, with a sprawling ego, who crisscrossed this country in railroad cars, piloted boats on the Mississippi River, and skidded the Atlantic and Pacific Oceans on ships, wrote nouns, verbs and adjectives on this desk between two Tiffany lamps. This was his *Shed*. Well, it was his main *Shed*. At his summer residence, Quarry Farm at Elmira, New York, Twain had a great little building called the Study, a gazebo, where he wrote. It was built for Twain by Susan and Theodore Crane in 1874. They built it for him so he could write undisturbed. It was a place built on a hill at Quarry Farm, which allowed cross ventilation to keep the place cool in the hot summer months. It was a simple building with a writing table, a few chairs, and a sofa. It was a place where he could stay connected to himself and write words on paper. Both the billiard room and the Study served as *Sheds* for Mark Twain throughout his literary career. Twain finished *Huckleberry Finn* in the Study, at Elmira in 1883. In time, my wife and I will take a trip to there to pay homage to this great man of letters.

Arthur Miller

As a high school student, a student of the theatre, and a teacher of theatre and literature, the common thread that I can trace through these disciplines, is Miller's play *Death of a Salesman*. This play, after all of my years dealing with it, still rattles me on many levels. In high school, I could relate to Biff. In college I wanted to play Biff onstage. As a parent I didn't want a Biff for a son, and I certainly didn't want to be Willy Loman as a father. Miller basically is telling us, in this play, to pay very close attention to our values. As I write this, I can hear Biff and Willy arguing, and it sends chills through me. If there is an author that I wish I could talk with about my *Shed* metaphor, it would be Arthur Miller.

Miller actually had a *Shed* built on his property, for the express purpose of writing *Death of a Salesman*. I remember teaching the play at school in the '80s, and reading somewhere that Miller had a real *Shed* where he'd write in his backyard. I didn't pay it much mind at that time; as of this writing however, it has tremendous significance.

The *Shed* was about 10x10, with a pitched roof maybe 12 feet high. It was an austere building painted white, with a door and four windows. It lay near the edge of the woods on his property. When Miller finished the play, and it was performed on stage, the original work was entitled, Inside Of His Head and actor Lee J. Cobb played Willy Loman. Also, Jo Mielziner designed a very innovative set, in order to deal with the hallucinatory experiences Willy was having during the play. This was not a fun night at the theatre, I'll guarantee you that. This play made audiences uneasy. If you could identify with Willy, you squirmed. If you were a corporate big shot, you squirmed (maybe not). If you identified with Biff, your blood pressure probably spiked, and you left the theatre. If you identified with Happy, well, you probably just didn't get it. If you identified with Linda, you wept. If you identified with Charley, you nodded like a wise sage. Miller did what writers are supposed to do, and that is to expand a reader's knowledge base, to make them feel something. He hit this one out of the ballpark.

Arthur Miller was born in Harlem, New York City, but then his family moved between Lenox and Fifth Avenues. Miller came from humble beginnings, his father was an illiterate Jewish immigrant from Poland, and his mother was teacher in the public school he attended. His father had a successful business that manufactured ladies-wear, but it was ruined in the Depression. This had a strong influence on the young Miller. He learned to move on, and reinvent himself. The family then moved to a small house in Brooklyn, which is said to be the model for the home in Death of a Salesman.

Miller was not a very good student, and failed many subjects; he flunked algebra three times. He was more interested in playing sports than school. He was not well read. A turning point in

Miller's unextraordinary youth of playing sports, and reading some adventure stories, came when he read *The Brothers Karamazov*, by Dostoevsky. After high school, he worked at an auto parts warehouse on Tenth Avenue in Manhattan. During that time he picked up Dostoevsky, thinking it was a detective story, and read it on the subway on his way to work. It was then that he decided to become a writer. His work ethic and tenacity rivals Twains. For two and a half years he saved thirteen dollars a week of the fifteen that he earned, in order to finance a year in college. He went on to study journalism at the University of Michigan in 1934, and won awards for playwriting. I mention this, because I felt as a teacher that there was always that one particular book which grabbed a person, sending them on a quest to expand their mind. I will not digress any further about Miller the student; I will stick to my task, and discuss the *Shed* metaphor, and how it relates to *Death of a Salesman*.

In a nutshell, this play deals with a guy who thinks he's a better success than he really is. He claims to be "well-liked," wherever he goes. His sons adore their dad. Willy's wife Linda, while believing in the American Dream, is a grounded woman. Willy is fired from his job, and his life begins to come unglued. Willy, like most people, is defined by what he does, not who he is. Ultimately, Willy's values are the cause of his undoing.

One scene that illustrates this is when Willy thinks that Biff's teacher will fudge a grade because he's a good football player. Willy sees Biff's future as a successful college graduate and businessman. Biff puts the name of the college he wants to attend on his sneakers, without any real concern about the work involved in getting into that school. Biff's values are further eroded, when he thinks that all he needs to do is have his dad go talk to his Math teacher. (You know, because he's Willy Loman.) Well, sometimes this kind of thing doesn't work out, at all. Things get worse for the family, when Biff, unexpectedly shows up to see his father in Boston, and finds him with another woman. From that point on, Biff sees his father as an empty suit, a liar, a cheat. In contrast to Biff's pain, his brother Happy goes on as if nothing happened and all is well in the Loman household.

Biff roams the country to try to find his place in the world, without much success. Willy just can't see why Biff can't come back to New York and set the business world on fire. Here lies the main conflict in the play. Willy may've been a good salesman, but Biff's not buying Willy's value system, and can see right through him. The most gut wrenching scenes in the play are between Biff and Willy in the kitchen, where Biff calls him out on his plan to harm himself, and Willy denies all of what he's saying. The intense dialogue is what all actors dream of doing, because of the heavy, emotional pull which drives this climactic scene. Then after the explosion of hard words between father and son, Biff says:

"No! Nobody's hanging himself, Willy! I ran down eleven flights with a pen in my hand today. And suddenly I stopped, you hear me? And in the middle of that office building, do you hear this? I stopped in the middle of that building and I saw—the sky. I saw the things that I love in this world. The work and the food and time to sit and smoke. And I looked at the pen and said to myself, what the hell am I grabbing this for? Why am I trying to become what I don't want to be? What am I doing in an office, making a contemptuous, begging fool of myself, when all I want is out there, waiting for me the minute I say I know who I am! Why can't I say that Willy?!"

The scene continues with Biff telling his father that he, Biff Loman, is not a leader of men, but a dime a dozen. Then, Willy says in an uncontrolled outburst:

"I am not a dime a dozen! I am Willy Loman and you are Biff Loman!"

At this cathartic moment in the scene Biff yells,

"I am nothing! I'm nothing, Pop! Can't you understand that? I'm just what I am, that's all."

It is no wonder to me that Arthur Miller built a *Shed* on his property to write this play. It seems that he stripped away all comfort in this simple building, to face the thematic demons. Literally and metaphorically, Miller must've stripped away all comfort. This is very uncomfortable for me to write about, simply as an observer of this great playwright; I can't imagine what Miller felt writing this manuscript. One thing I'll bet my last nickel on, is that this play was exhausting for him to write.

In the Requiem of the play, Miller spells it all out for us through the words of Biff and the Loman's neighbor Charley.

Biff: There were a lot of nice days. When he'd come home from a trip; or on Sundays, making a stoop; finishing the cellar; putting on the new porch; when he built the extra bathroom; and put up the garage. You know something, Charley, there's more of him in that front stoop, than in all the sales he ever made.

Charley: Yeah, he was a happy man with a batch of cement.

Linda: He was so wonderful with his hands.

Biff: He had the wrong dreams. All, all wrong.

Miller has Biff say the following line twice in the Requiem: "He never knew who he was."

Willy Loman didn't know where or what his *Shed* was.

Arthur Miller's play challenged his audience with a very tough question. He forced people to examine their values. Obviously, he believed that families could be destroyed by false values. Willy believed in the Horatio Alger version of the American Dream or in Willy's mind, the American Promise. For all of his faults, Willy meant well. He didn't try to hurt anyone. Miller shows us through Willy Loman that we all have a responsibility to do as Socrates said, "Know Thy Self," or as this author would say "Know Thy "Shed." "

Nota Bene: This play, *Death of a Salesman*, written in the small, unpretentious *Shed* in Arthur Miller's backyard, opened on Broadway in 1949, and ran for 742 performances.

Contemporaries

Now that the heavy lifting is done with the aforementioned, and what I perceive to be their Sheds, I'll move forward with some contemporary artists and others, and explore what or where their Sheds are. By this time in this little book, it is my hope that you are beginning to think of what or where your Shed is.

"To Thine own Shed be True."
J. V. Houlihan, Jr.

Tim Philbrick

Tim Philbrick says, "When I try to describe a piece of furniture with good proportions, I immediately think of the Newport secretaries that were made in the 1750s. The careful layout of the immense facades on these masterpieces might be called the definition of balance and harmony. The success of these revered pieces is not accidental. They were made by craftsman who learned to build furniture using classical proportioning systems. Some of these systems, drawn from nature and religion, have been with us for 5000 years."

This is a glimpse into the mind of Tim, the furniture designer who I spoke of earlier. Tim's *Shed* is literally in his house, which was built in 1905. The space, which has a view of the ocean, was originally a carriage house. I asked Tim, as I've asked many artists I've met in my life, "How did this all start?" (I posed this question to an architect I know, who is a Professor at M I T once. He said, "Well, my aunt had a small grocery store, and in the back there were empty boxes, and I started messing around with them." Then he said, "I started building tree houses." Interesting huh, from empty boxes, and tree houses, to designing buildings all over the world. (Go figure this stuff.)

Tim said that his dad had a work bench in the basement of their summer home in Wellfleet, Massachusetts. "It was a simple bench with a few tools: dull handsaws, dull planes, a hammer, a screwdriver or two." He also added that his dad, a poet, and a professor at Brown University at that time, had a *Shed* at the Wellfleet summerhouse where he wrote. His dad called it the "Shack." Charles Philbrick authored four books of poetry, and a children's book about his four sons. Tim showed me a copy of a book of his dad's poems, with a picture of the "Shack" on the back cover. It was like Arthur Miller's, very simple and austere. Tim also showed me a half model of a sailboat hull that his dad made.

When Tim was about ten, father and son embarked on a project in the garage, to build something called a *"Folboat."* According to the advertisement, it was so easy to build that, "Two co-eds could build one in their dorm room." Tim said it wasn't that easy, but after "Lots of dad's cursing, and many beers later," the boat was finished, and was used for many years by he and his brothers. Tim has come a long way from the *"Folboat." He* points out a poster of a cross section of a Steinway Piano. "I built three art case pianos for Steinway." Tim moves casually through his Shed, with Anita O' Day and Ray Eldridge's cool jazz wafting through the air, and he seems to barely have a pulse. Indeed, a garage boat project, to a Steinway Piano, Tim Philbrick surely has come a long way.

Tim found himself in San Francisco, after an independent study of Sufism a (type of mysticism) during his final year of high school.

He'd recently bought a slew of antiques from Rhode Island, and with his brother, drove out west to sell them. Their shop was called Mt. Ararat. Pretty heady stuff I'd say. Tim's dad's subsequent illness brought him back to Rhode Island, where he felt it was time to apply himself, and focus on something to perhaps make a career of. This was when he met an old Swamp Yankee named Johnny Northup. Tim apprenticed with Northup for four years. The first thing he learned from his mentor was how to turn a pedestal on a lathe for a Candle Stand table. It took Northup about five minutes to turn one of these things on his lathe; it took Tim about an hour. Before Tim moved on four years later, he could turn them as fast, or faster than Northup. He felt he'd learned all he could at that time from his mentor, and this awareness, led him to Boston University.

When he arrived at BU, Tim met John Kirk, the Head of "The American Studies Department," where Tim was interested in studying. In the middle of a crowded building of students, the following conversation took place.

John Kirk asked Tim, "Do you want to be in the Graduate, or Undergraduate section of the class."

"What's the difference?"

"Well, there's a test."

"When can I take the test?"

"Right now."

"OK."

Kirk opens up his briefcase, and pulls out two 8x10 photographs and says, "One of these is a period Chippendale Chair, and the other is a Centennial reproduction (these reproductions were popular in the 1870s). Here's the test, which is which, and why."

"That's easy," Tim replied. "The one on the left is a Boston Chippendale with beautiful deep carving; the one on the right is the Centennial reproduction, identifiable by its shallow, lifeless carving."

"You're in," said Kirk.

Thus began Tim's academic career, and the life of a furniture designer.

According to Tim, "It is true that many proportioning systems have acquired degrees of complexity, but the basic principle is simple: in order for a piece to be balanced and harmonious, each part must relate to the whole." Sounds to this layman, and a cockeyed cutter of wood—I'd measure three times, and still cut the wood poorly—like Tim's talking about Buckminster Fuller's concept of "Synergy," but what the hell do I know.

As I walk through Tim's *Shed*, I see so many tools of various functions. He tried to explain the uses of them, and my eyes started crossing and I felt a migraine coming on, so I'll simply list them: myriad clamps for gluing things from one inch to six feet, spoke shaves, in shaves (one in the shape of a whale), block planes (several), hammers, levels, tri-squares, drawknives, rabbit planes, dovetail, back, and veneer saws, mortise gauges, awls, miter gauges, dividers, assorted glues, routers of various sizes (a very important tool, according to Tim), drill bits (several), files of many shapes and functions, grinders, chisels, measuring implements, a micrometer (I'm clueless), squares and indicators, assorted screws, pencils, a 19th century dill press with a flat leather belt drive, and lathes. I picked up an ornate piece of wood, and said, "What's this?"

"A finial for a bedpost," he said.

"Oh that's nice," I said, not really knowing what a finial was.

Tim said it was just a mock up. He was making a bed for a cousin, and was mocking around ideas (pun intended). "There are only so many possible ideas for a finial, and I was trying to make it not look like a Pagoda or a penis."

"Oh I see," I said.

We walked over to Tim's desk, which he built while at BU, the chair was also built at that time. I sat down and looked at the desk where he does his designs. To the right, there's a wall full of memorabilia from his past openings and shows. I looked out the window, and admired the view, and ambient light. "So this is where you do your designing eh, Tim?"

"Well, kind of," he said, and went on to explain how a piece evolves from a discussion with a client, and a drawing (remember the "balance, proportion and harmony" stuff?), and this is where his art, and his "Shed" reveals itself. Tim explained the process very simply.

He said he'll first discuss with a client what they're looking for regarding the piece, and see what their aesthetic is. Then, if possible, he'll go to the space where the, let's say, chair will sit. Once that's established, he'll make a drawing to scale the piece. "Then," he says grabbing a box, "I'll let them look at these." In the box was a bunch of samples: Macassar Ebony, Sapele, Swiss Pear Wood (Tim's favorite), Dark Indian Rosewood, Figured Claro, Walnut, and Maracaibo Boxwood. So, after all of this is agreed upon, Tim begins to make the piece, in his *Shed*.

According to Tim, "Perhaps the most elaborate, and widely studied proportioning systems are the five classic orders of architecture developed in ancient Greece and Rome. Although designed as a set of rules for architects, the orders of architecture became a proportional framework for furniture designers beginning in the Renaissance. Both Thomas Chippendale, and Thomas Sheraton, began their 18th century design books with elaborate studies of the five orders. Sheraton devoted thirty pages to this subject."

I'll go out on a limb here, and say that Tim will make you one hell of a chair. Here's another example of how this guy's mind works. "In furniture, the ratios of height to width to depth are the first relationships to resolve, and the human body usually will determine at least one of these measurements. For example, most of us find chair seats of about seventeen inches high comfortable and dining tables of about thirty inches high appropriate." (I never really gave these kinds of numbers a second thought, until I started talking to Tim Philbrick.)

Getting back to the Steinway Pianos, I looked closer at the poster on the wall of Tim's *Shed*. I noticed that there was a whole list of piano nomenclature at the bottom of the picture of this work of art. Things like: Underlayer top flanges, Damper wire screws, Leg buttons, Balancier coverings et al. Needless to say, this is a complex work of art. As I was taking notes about the Steinway, Tim mentioned another very important tool in his *Shed*, and that was a humidifier. "It's very important to keep the humidity and temperature as constant as possible." I guess that when you making a case for a Steinway, you better have all of your ducks in a row. Some other little tools Tim showed me were some twenty-two caliber bullets in a box near his files and screws. "What are these for," I asked.

"Woodchucks, they get into our garden, and they're a real nuisance."

Nota Bene: Tim sits patiently on the roof of his *Shed*, with a single shot rifle to deal with these critters.

One day I gave Tim some scrap teak that I had left over from a job done on my sailboat/*Shed*. I'd hired a Newport carpenter to make me some new teak hatch boards, and there was some new teak, plus the old hatch boards left over, and I figured Tim could use them to make something. So I brought the wood into his *Shed*, and there ensued a discussion about teak. I wanted to know the best and easiest way to care for the teak on my boat. Tim said oiling it twice a year would keep it looking good. He picked up the new piece of scrap teak, and showed me little streaks of white stuff. "See this Joe," he said pointing to the barely noticeable streaks, "these are mineral deposits and they can dull the blades of my table saw." I couldn't believe such a minute amount of a mineral could actually do damage to a blade. "No teak allowed in my *Shed*," Tim said laughing. Again, Tim demonstrated how he understood the constituents of his *Shed*, from the vast array of his tools, right down to minimal amounts of minerals in a piece of teak.

Finally, Tim likes to listen to music in his *Shed*. He has a love of Jazz, and is extremely fond of the Rhode Island's own *Roomful of Blues*, especially the earlier stuff. Again, I'll simply list the titles because like his tools, they're too hard to place in any climactic order. Tim listens too: Al Basile, a former trumpet player with *Roomful of Blues*. (Al has many CDs to his credit.) Joe Liggins *The Shuffle Boogie King*, Louis Jordan, *Blues Shouter* Wynonie Harris, Roy Eldridge the *Little Jazz Trumpet Giant*, (Eldridge encouraged Rhode Islander Scott Hamilton, a Tenor Saxophone player to come to New York, as a young man; it changed Scott's life...remember the mentor thing?) Count Basie, Dinah Washington. This is a partial list. I note one title called *Boogie Uproar*, and wonder if Tim rocks out: fingers popping, head bopping and feet tapping, in the privacy of his *Shed*, while making a table, chair or Steinway Piano.

Nota Bene: After the last interview session in Tim Philbrick's *Shed*, I noticed a finished chair covered in plastic, cushioned with red Italian Calf Skin. It looked like a work of art, with "balance, proportion and harmony."

Mark Holden

At the age of four, he was dragging his dad's drum kit to gigs in the City of Newport, the next thing he knew, he was banging drums. When Mark Holden was in the first grade, he come home from school and draw sailboats as precisely as he could; multi-decked powerboats also. As a young teen, Mark would fish golf balls out of the water hazards at the local golf course; clean them, package them, and then sell them. As I write about Mark Holden's *Shed*, or shall I say *Sheds*, the reader needs this prior knowledge:

The following contains some genealogy that led Mark Holden to one of his *Sheds*.

Charles S. Barnum

<u>Newport Mercury</u> *November 9, 1861*

"It was with feelings of deep regret we learned of the unfortunate accident in our bay on Tuesday last, by which Mr. Charles S. Barnum, of this city, with two other companions, lost their lives. Mr. Barnum, of this city, had been to Providence to ship a crew for the brig *F. F. Newton*, and on his passage down the river with a party of eight in a sailboat, a squall struck the sail, which was fastened, and capsized the boat. Mr. Barnum's body did not sink, and was picked up by the schooner *Mail*, who also rescued four of the party that clung to the sailor's chests, which floated after the boat sunk, and one was rescued by a boat from Prudence Island.

The deceased was admirably calculated for his situation in life with a large family depending on his exertions for their support, his happy disposition seldom allowed his spirits to falter. Thus buoyed up, he managed to maintain his family by the income derived from his agency in shipping seamen, keeping an intelligence office, supplying vessels with water from his water boat, and when all these failed to furnish employment for the moment, he might be found at his cobblers bench always cheerful, never desponding; in a word; we know of no man in the community who moves in so humble a sphere as did C.S. Barnum, who would be missed so much as he is. But in the community his place will be filled by others, to his family the loss is irreparable, and we hope the widow overburdened with sorrow and care as she is, may not fail to receive the sympathy and aid which is so needful at the present moment."

<u>Barnum Charles S. Shipping Intelligence Office, 1 Ferry Wharf. Home 165 Thames St.</u>

Mark Holden is the Dock Master, of the Newport Harbor Hotel and Marina, aka, The Treadway, at 1 Ferry Wharf. To imagine Mark's great-great-great-grandfather, Charles S. Barnum, working on the very docks and streets that Mark now works, gives this author pause, and the idea of genetics takes the fore. Mark showed me the obituary. I read it and was transfixed as he said, "Just think Joe, one hundred and twenty years ago plus, my great-great-great-grandfather looked out toward Goat Island, and this very harbor, at all of the comings and goings just as we are now, and I basically do what he did." Thanks to the internet, Mark was able to track down this little nugget of genealogy, which is germane to one of Mark's *Sheds*. Moreover, the kind words written about Charles S. Barnum, could easily be said by this author regarding Mark; you'll be hard pressed to find a nicer guy on the waterfront and on the water of Newport Harbor. I could provide testimony, but just trust me on this one.

Boats

Mark Holden is very familiar with Newport Harbor. He remembers going out on the boat *King Tut* with his father, who played drums in a Dixieland band. They would greet the America's Cup racing sailboats (the Twelve Meters) off Castle Hill, as they came back into the harbor after a day of racing. "Just being on or near the water was enough," he says. When he was a young kid, he asked his parents if they could buy a flagpole; not for patriotic reasons, he just wanted to hear the halyard slapping against the pole. This is something that can annoy sailors at anchor, to Mark however, it was music (rhythm actually, a drumming sound: rat, tat, tat tat tat tat; notice how the author snared you into that cadence...). Mark's eleventh grade English teacher was building a boat in the backyard, and since he was pals with the teacher's son, he ended up fetching things to help the guy build his boat.

Fast forward to Mark living aboard his 1939 Alden sloop called *Luau*—built in City Island, New York—in the anchorage off King's

Park in Newport. He lived aboard, in this anchorage, on the hook (anchor), for five years. At that time he was also playing drums in a Rock and Roll band. He says of his Alden, "While Hitler was invading Poland, people may've been drinking tea aboard this boat. If these cabin walls could talk, huh?!" Mark has a passion for things of the past. "I remember humping my drum kit to do gigs on Block Island. I could smell cigarette smoke and spilled beer from every bar in Newport that my dad played, back in his Rock and Roll band days." Mark's a third generation drummer. I've heard recordings of bands that he's played in, and the guy doesn't drop a note. The Holden family currently lives aboard a fifty-foot trawler called *Bliss*. Mark Holden is a man of many *Sheds*.

Drums

"When I'm performing, it is complete freedom, like when you leave the dock in your boat and you're free." As stated earlier, Mark is a third generation drummer. Mark's a handsome mild mannered guy; but behind the drum kit he's a sweating primate, beating the kit into submission. I've heard his earlier Rock and Roll work with the band *Outnumbered*, a cover band, and *Seducer*, a band that did all original material. Currently, a Country and Western band called *The Gillies* is where Mark is hitting pure rhythm shots: rat tat tat. Any way you want it played, this guy will do it. His musicianship is clearly evident in the *Gillies*' recordings. "One of my other *Sheds* is the studio," Mark says. "Working with guys and ladies who look at the music studio as their *Shed* makes the band create on a powerful level."

I met Mark five years ago, when I decided to keep my boat in wet storage in Newport for the winter. We'd hang around his Dock Master's office, talking about boats, music, and books. After becoming fast friends, Mark shared with me one of his inventions. He developed a product for drummers to use that helped keep the sticks adhered to the hand. He invented the product while living aboard his *Shed* at the time, *Luau*. It became apparent to me that this guy had a "thinking outside of the box" thing going on, and that he was clearly marching to the beat of a "different drummer." Mark is what you'd call a guy who tinkers with things. "I just always want to make something better," he says smiling. "I'm a re-inventor."

The Red *Shed*

A few years ago Mark wanted to make his own bio-fuel. At that time he was living in Bristol Rhode Island in a house with his family. Gone were the live aboard days of a single sailorman/musicman. His wife thought it would be a good idea if he built a *Shed* in the backyard to fabricate his bio-fuel apparatus, rather than do this in the basement. "In about three days, I had a 9x15 science lab with two doors, and a window with a flower box." A week later he ran enough electricity to his *Red Shed*, to power a small town. "It was a cross between a tree house and a land yacht." It became the closest thing to a boat that he could construct, so that he could work on his projects. Mark is a "Whatever It Takes," kind of guy.

I got some insight into Mark's inventiveness, when one day at the Dock Master's office he started telling me about Thomas Edison's lab down in Florida. Edison's neighbor was Henry Ford, and both men were constantly bouncing ideas off each other. Mark's eyes bulged as he described what Edison's work space looked like. "He had a bunk right in his lab, so he could sleep if need be!" Mark said this with great enthusiasm. I never met a guy who got so amped up about Thomas Edison.

He continued on about his bio-fuel apparatus, and the chemical constituents of its ingredients. "My *Red Shed* now smelled like a bad day at a McDonald's." He would siphon off grease collected from restaurants in Newport, and run them through copper pipes connected to a hot water heater. "It looked like a robot," he said. He described his make shift hazardous material suit and the look on his wife's face, the day a tractor trailer pulled up to his house, and off- loaded a fifty-five gallon drum with a skull and crossbones on the barrel.

Mark had a blue oar over the entrance of the *Red Shed*, and it's a perfect metaphor for Mark the inventor. He says it was once a healthy set of oars, but someone stole one from his dinghy. "After a gig one night, I was on my way out to my sailboat, and noticed an oar was missing, so I fashioned a broom into the oarlock, and made my way slow and steady, over the hundred yards it took to get to *Luau*." Here's a guy who made the best with what he had to work with, and moved forward to his goal; as all inventors must do. "I could never give up that oar," he says with conviction. This is a man, who will not give up on his dream. He will stay close to his *Sheds*.

Salty Paws

Another business Mark ventured into was a place on Thames Street in Newport called "Salty Paws." It was kind of a snazzy pet store. He told me of an idea he had for a doggie treat called "Fido Castro." One night he found himself rolling out dough at the kitchen table, into what looked like cigars. He baked them, and then fashioned a little label on them. Next he figured he'd build a little humidor, and lay the treats in the box. Thus was born the little cigar doggie treat (dogs loved them) called "Fido Castro." His logo was a dog with a Fidel Castro kind of hat, with the treat in his mouth. Demand increased immediately, and the problem now was where to bake the cigar treats. He knew a guy who owned a restaurant, and the guy let him come in at night and bake the cigars after eleven. So here's Mark, baking away and trying to stay ahead of the demand. I can only imagine the look on his wife's face, as Mark went out to bake "Fido Castro's" at eleven. The product was very successful. "Oprah's secretary found out about the product, and wanted some," he said ruefully, "it was a case of supply and demand, and I just couldn't keep up the pace." Mark had learned his lesson regarding supply and demand.

An offshoot of his drummer's grip product was his development of *Voodoo Grip*, for baseball bats. The Dodgers are currently using this product for their team. "If high school and college baseball teams pick up on "Voodoo Grip", I'll hit the ground running. There will be a ready supply of product. I won't get Fido Castroed again." Mark Holden is a man that can't help himself with his desire to "make things better;" it's simply the way he's hard wired.

Several years back while he worked at Vanguard Boats, a company responsible for making small fiberglass sailboats, he decided to make a surfboard. After that design was completed, he made carbon fiber drum shells for himself. "I just can't turn it off, I always want to design and reinvent and refine." Whether it's discussing boats, music, or bio-diesel, you can see the drive, focus and passion in this guy's eyes. He is always in one of his *Sheds*.

So as Mark Holden works the docks, and walks the streets of Newport, as his great-great-great grandfather Charles S. Barnum did all those years ago, he feels a sense of things being temporary. "We're all just passing through," he says. As he looks to the west from his office on the docks, I can see his wheels are turning. I realize at that moment, that whichever of his *Sheds* he's working in, Mark Holden will press on working at "making things better."

Cameron Greenlee

"It seems that a *Shed* is vital within everyone's life: artists, businessmen, cooks and athletes. Everyone needs somewhere they can go for refuge, to be comfortable, to get into the right head space." This is Cameron Greenlee's take on what a *Shed* is. Block Island, Rhode Island, is one of Cam's *Sheds*. Since his youth, racing dinghies and keelboats, and rolling down the twisting bends of Coast Guard Road, Cam has connected with this island. "It was here that I came to develop a clear understanding of who I was as a young man."

Cameron is a very personable guy with a genuine winning smile. I remember seeing Cam with his parents at the ferry docks when the family came from City Island, New York, to Block Island. I remember talking with his dad, Dr. Bob Greenlee, about sailing; he always seemed to have a small sailboat in tow, while his kids were in the car waiting to board the ferry, many years ago. Cam's family has had property on the island at Cormorant Cove since the 1960s. Their home was built in the 1980s. Cam has spent the last ten summers, falls, and some winter seasons on Block Island.

Cameron Greenlee has a strong connection to Block Island. He remembers walking his grandparent's dog Honey along the island's roads. He read his grandfather's manuscripts that journal the celestial navigation calculations that dealt with the rising tides at Seal Rock. He witnessed breathtaking sunsets that developed him spiritually. "It has all been such a large part of what has formed my life as a Spirit Soldier." Block Island is one of Cameron's *Sheds*.

His musical discipline evolved on the island. Cam would host jam sessions, and write new songs on Block Island; playing piano is a big part of Cam's life. A friend of his, Joe Curran, says, "After surfing, Cam would sit down and get lost at the keyboard before dinner. We'd have to yell at him that dinner was ready, ya know, total absorption."

Horace said something like this, "One can go from one place to another and it changes the heavens but not the soul." More simply stated it means, "Wherever you go, there you are." Cam, because of his need to expand as a professional musician, needed to leave Block Island. He ended up in New York City with its cold and windy streets. Moreover, he's had to become a "Road Warrior," to advance with his musical career. Cameron augments his income by working on various boat projects. One of our interview sessions involved me handing off some questions and a small tape recorder as Cam was heading off to Newport to do some work on a seventy-foot Little Harbor sailboat. We met in Newport two days later to continue talking, since the next day he was heading back to New York. Then, he was off to Australia and New Zealand to play keyboards with an iconic Reggae/Ska band called the *Skatalites*. Indeed, Cam Greenlee is a "Road Warrior."

Cam started playing piano at the age of five. He credits his supportive parents. "They wouldn't let me quit when I was about eleven," he says. "It was a time where I didn't think it was cool playing the piano." He spoke very highly of his parent's unwavering support over the years, for his musical ambitions. Over dinner, I casually asked Cam if he could play stuff by Dvorak. "Yup," he said. I asked about a few other classical guys, and he answered "Yup." He says that he looked at Mozart as someone to aspire to be like. He saw Mozart from a romantic point of view, as a great composer who traveled all over Europe performing his music for large audiences. At this point of the interview, I connected the musical dots between Classic musical training and Reggae, and started to think of the serious, humble nature of this young man who sat across from me.

The Boathouse/Block Island

"A *Shed* for me is a place where I feel comfortable; I can't create in a place where I'm not comfortable." The "Boathouse," on Block Island was built by Cam's grandparents, who were serious ocean cruising sailors, with several Atlantic crossings to their credit. They sailed to Block Island in the '60s, and decided to buy a piece of property on Cormorant Cove. It is there that they built the "Boathouse," and this is where Cam felt most comfortable, and developed creatively for ten years. "It's my spiritual home," he says. This unique structure, built on stilts at the water's edge, also has a dock. It's no wonder that he refers to this place as his "spiritual home." The boathouse is an artist's dream space, and Cam understands the value of this. It has driven his system of values, and a sense of responsibility.

This building served Cam's grandparents as a base camp of sorts as their main house was built in 1980. It had eighteen foot wide windows facing the water. Inside, the "Boathouse" was an austere space, serving literally as a shed to store and service small sailboats. (Remember I mentioned Dr. Bob Greenlee at the ferry dock with sailboats in tow?) It was also a place for guests to stay. It had couches and a small kitchen, and some small bunk rooms. "Nothing sophisticated at all," says Cam. The rafters spanned the building, where masts, hulls, and sail bags could be stored, "We're kind of a boat fanatic family. At any given time there can be as many as ten small hulls around the property," Cam says. As he tells me about this special space, I try to imagine the music that was played, written, and felt there. Also, I can imagine boat projects in progress.

I'd love a *Shed*, like this myself; I'm almost jealous. On a more serious note, I sense a monastic aspect to Cam's personality; he calls himself a "Spirit Soldier" for a reason. Furthermore, I begin to see more clearly the conflict Cam has with his nomadic career as a musician. As he speaks of this place, I see that he truly misses the environs, and his friends on Block Island.

Conserfest/Stewardship/Alternative Sheds

Nota Bene: My position regarding a person's *Shed* is that once a person finds out what or where their *Shed* is, there is a responsibility for the individual to take care of it. I know this may sound somewhat professorial, perhaps even didactic, but it must be stated at this point in Cameron's chapter. It's also a great place to support my thesis (the teacher thing again), and drive home a very important point: being a steward of our *Shed*.

Cameron has a Block Island boyhood friend Justin; whose grandfather, Captain Rob Lewis started the Block Island Conservancy back in the 1970s. Captain Lewis was a man of vision, and he knew that Block Island, a very unique place ecologically, needed attention paid to it regarding issues of land acquisition for conservation, and development. Cameron, Justin, Joe Curran and other friends decided to do what they could do to contribute to Captain Rob's legacy. (Again, I see a serious and conscientious side of Cam Greenlee, as he speaks of this special island which shaped the building blocks of his personality.)

Being a musician, he figured "Conserfest," would be a way that he could expand awareness of what Captain Lewis did many years ago, and make it accessible to the upcoming generation. Thus "Conserfest," a small music festival, was born in 2008. It started with humble, grassroots beginnings, and has grown steadily. "We actually have some money due to local support and contributions, and hopefully in 2010 more people will come out, and it will be bigger and better." Cam feels a need to give something back. "So you need to give something away to keep it," I say as a wise old sage noting this paradox (just joking). "Exactly," says Cam. He understands the sense of stewardship about "One of the Last Great Places," Block Island, one of Cam Greenlee's *Sheds*.

Being on the road these days with the *Skatalittes* requires an inordinate amount of traveling. Cam has played with this great band on four continents. "We played a gig in Siberia, about ten miles from Kathazkstan," Cam says casually. After the Australian tour, it's off to Japan with the *Skatalittes*. This group of musicians hails from Jamaica, where it originally formed in 1964. It was the original backup band for Bob Marley, Jimmy Cliff, and Peter Tosh. These seasoned professionals tour the world making great music. Cam joined the band in June 2009.

"I have to make do with a variety of *Sheds*. Anywhere that I can sit down for a minute and play a piano, to clear my mind, will always be a *Shed* for me." He also says his car can be a *Shed*. "I have time to think while I drive; I'm quite a thinker." This "Road Warrior" needs psychic space in order to create. The combination of Cam's love of music, sailing, and the ocean in general, appears to be a bittersweet mixture of passions. Surfing is also a passion of Cam's. This "in the moment" Zen mind activity is a natural fit for his personality. This is yet another comfortable *Shed*, for him to let his mind expand, flow and create.

Recently, Cam returned from a tour with the Skatalittes in Australia and New Zealand. He was promoting his new CD, *Cameron and the Trenton St. Collaborative*, produced by Naya Records. They were on a fast paced three night tour starting in Boston, then Newport, and ending in New York City. Then Cam would be off, as stated earlier, to Japan with the *Skatalittes*. I went to the Newport gig, and saw Cam work in his music *Shed*. This collection of young, vibrant, and schooled musicians led by Cam, scrambled the mind molecules, bones, and muscle fiber of all in attendance. To see and hear such expert musicianship roiling through explosive syncopated Jamaican rhythms: bass drums, horns, guitar and keyboards devouring the room, was something to behold. Cam is a centered guy, who moves with a sense of calm, but, when he plays his instrument, his passion and power come out of the tips of his fingers with focused determination and purpose. (These sentences may appear hyperbolic, but I assure you there is no hyperbole here.) In fact, I'll dare anyone to try and stay still while listening to this music. They played instrumentals while the audience bopped, hooted and howled—homage as it were—to these talented players. I saw Cam popping out of his seat with enthusiasm during the band's set. I saw Cam giving all of the players their time to shine during their solos. I saw Cam creating something very powerful and "in the moment," in his *Shed*, without restraint, and devoid of ego. I saw Cam's slender, trained and assertive fingers flourishing across the keyboard, and not dropping a note. I heard primitive howls coming out of Cam Greenlee's being. I saw a guy who loved being, and transcending in his *Shed*. The important verb is "being," not doing.

Jane Musky

"As a kid, I drew all of the time," says Jane Musky laughing. Jane's father was a classically trained musician, and she feels lucky to have grown up in such a creative environment. "My brothers and I all played many different instruments, and of course I also drew," she says laughing again. Jane Musky is a Production Designer in the film business. "I designed my first play in the fifth grade, and that was the first time I learned that I could take an existing space and turn it into something else." Jane's laughter is very revealing in regards to her art. This woman clearly loves her work, and more importantly, knows what her *Shed* is.

A Production Designer is an integral part of the filmmaking process. When I myself was a theatre student in college, I learned this firsthand while banging nails backstage. I heard the set designer confer with painters, carpenters, costume designers and lighting people, about what was needed for the actors, and most importantly, the requirements of the script. Jane's job on a film project involves working closely with the director, producer, and director of photography. This collaboration allows the visual feel, tone, and aesthetic of the film to evolve, hopefully into a great experience for the audience. Once called Art Directors, the titled changed to Production Designer, after a guy named Cameron Menzies did an inordinate amount of work, alone, on *Gone with the Wind*.

Jane's formal training started in high school in New Jersey. "There were always school plays being produced, musicals, and other smaller stuff." She was involved in an Art Major program, now known as an Advanced Placement Art Program. It was one of the first A P Art Programs of this kind in the country. She designed all of the sets for the plays and musicals at school, and she was blessed with having very sophisticated teachers, who saw she was very capable, and who encouraged her to expand and grow. These teachers saw that designing was Jane's forte, and pointed her into the direction which would serve her art. After her acceptance at Pratt Institute and some other Fine Art colleges, she decided to attend the Boston University College of Fine Arts. There, she attended the Theatre School as a scenic design major. "Boston University has always had a formidable program in theatre design," says Jane. So began a four year program of study to become a professional designer for the theatre. Jane, the freshman at Boston University, was on the way to her future in the theatre and film business.

Jane Musky speaks impeccable English, punctuated with laughter when talking about her work. Her smile is genuine and contagious, but her laughter is noteworthy. "When I'm designing something, it feels exciting," she says. "I'm taking an idea and building it from the ground up." She also notes that design is all around her and she can rearrange things. "What I like about movies is that you pull into Santa Fe, New Mexico, let's say, and turn it into a 1880s town." She notes that she makes broad strokes to create a visual experience. It becomes very clear at this point in my interview with Jane, that she truly has the eye of a visual artist.

While at BU, Jane became a very good scene painter. She could paint scenery for plays and opera, and was able to make a living doing that. She worked in London for two years painting drops for the English National Opera. "Scene painting became a calling card of mine. Not only could I make money, but people loved my painting, so I met some great designers because of that skill." While looking for her own work, she was mentored by some famous designers, absorbing and assimilating what they knew. "I was able to talk with these talented designers while I was painting their sets." I'm sure it was apparent to these people that Jane Musky was the type of person who was willing to immerse herself in whatever artistic project she was involved with. These people knew what Jane's *Shed* was.

Things are a little different these days for Jane the Production Designer. "My job is a team effort. I have about one hundred people who work with me on a film—carpenters, set dressers, scene painters." She has an immediate staff which draws up all of the sets and does all of the graphics for the movies that she designs now. "It's a very harmonious group that's worked together for a long time." Jane likes working with the same people because she feels that they just keep getting better and better. "We can talk to each other in shorthand now." The more I talk with Jane about the design process, the more I realize how little I know—and I actually studied theatre arts in college. Furthermore, I realize that she has many tools in her *Shed*. "I feel a sense of freedom and autonomy when I'm designing movies; it's all about me and how I see things. I'm very lucky. I just dream up ideas, and then have to make sense of them and spend money on them." She likens beginning a theatre production or a movie with "whiteness," like a blank canvas.

The Art Department Studio space, beside an empty sound stage, is what Jane considers her *Shed*. She says, "At the starting gate of a movie, it's a great moment when the team all gets together and discusses where we are going with the work ahead of us." (All of these creative people in one *Shed* must ratchet up the production value of the film.) Jane says that, "We're all standing at our tables getting out our drawing kits, and everyone's paper racks are bare." She adds, "It's a powerful feeling when we begin to build this great monolithic set, and that there will be two to three hundred plates of drawing when the movie's done." The amount of work Jane speaks of seems daunting. She talks about timetables, budgets, and long days during production. Moreover, she says that her set decorator is a very important part of her team. This person is responsible for the large and small elements of a particular set.

Two particular films Jane designed, *Finding Forrester*, and *Glengarry Glen Ross* (which are favorites of mine), have subtle little touches for their set designs. In the exposition of *Finding Forrester*, we see a slow pan of the book titles that belong to Jamal, one of the main characters. In Forrester's apartment, we see earthy wood tones, tables crammed with books, and an old typewriter. These elements are germane to each of these characters. This is what

Jane does for the film. In David Mamet's play, *Glengarry Glen Ross*, which was adapted as a movie, we see a more stage designed set; the blocking (movement) of the actors in this film looks very much like a staged production. I'm sure the director and Jane shared notes, in regard to this aesthetic, in pre-production meetings. I saw these films years before I knew that Jane was the designer, or who she was for that matter. However, I see the stamp of her art, especially the paint tones, in these films. It is clear in seeing Jane's film work, how she utilizes her tools, metaphorically speaking—all of the creative people on her team—in the creation of a movie.

All of Jane's film credits are too extensive to mention, so I'll mention a few recent ones: *Hitch, Music and Lyrics,* and, *The Bounty Hunter*. Most recently, Jane was working on a film entitled, *Something Borrowed*. I went to the corners of Varrick and Washington Streets in the West Village in New York City, and it was here that I saw Jane Musky in her *Shed*, doing what she loves to do most; design movies.

Jane was working within the walls of one of the largest footprints for a building in New York City. The Art Department for this film had set up camp here, to create the set for what Jane referred to as a "small film." To see Jane in her *Shed* was very revealing. This woman was clearly in her element, and her smile lit up the space. Jane had just got in from another location off the West Side Highway, where they would be shooting that night. An artist came into her office with some graphic art (a decal) for the side of a helicopter, which would be used in one of the shots. Jane told the artist, "Great job." She also told the young guy about making sure the helicopter people were OK with putting the art on the aircraft. "Sometimes they're a little picky about putting things on the helicopters because of the paint." Jane carries herself with a casual multi-tasking assertiveness. Furthermore, she makes her job look easy. (While talking about the design of the film, she was scanning a catalogue looking for a bed for her daughter's apartment.) She showed me the initial drawings of the sets at her drawing board, and pointed out where other artists had their work stations.

We walked to the carpentry, paint, and property shops, and I noted that all of the people were busily on task. I also saw a woman in the wardrobe room rummaging through piles of clothing. Jane explained that they were wrapping up shooting in two weeks. "Then we'll break all of this down, pack it up and move on to something else. It's like a Rock and Roll show," she said smiling. It seemed like a monumental task for a "small film." My host seemed unfazed by the immensity of the work which I perceived. Jane led me up a ramp and into the main set of the main character, her apartment. We were transported into a very comfortable living space. It was a small studio type apartment with lots of feminine energy: warm paint tones and fabrics, and huge hair curlers. As Jane explained things about the character that lived here, it became clear that all of the furniture, books, food, etc. were, as in *Finding Forrester*, germane to who this person is. I noticed through window lots of shrubs, vines and other plants. These were all part of Jane's vision for this set. She also explained how the walls could break away, if the cameramen, directors, makeup, continuity people, and grips needed space to film the actors. This was Jane's domain, her vision and design, and it all started with a blank sheet of paper—in her *Shed*. But way before this moment in time, I thought this all began with a young kid who, "drew all of the time."

Jane had been in the Hamptons working on this film. The production company rented a house, and recreated the interior to serve the character's needs. Jane showed me some false restaurant and bar signs she'd designed, to go over the real signs of the locations in which they were also shooting. (I always knew that films were not literal, and that you could cheat a little in creating different locations.) All of this effort is required for a film to work, and Jane Musky is in the vortex of this maelstrom of creative energy.

After the tour of Jane's *Shed*, I felt a new awareness of the responsibility of her job. There was a substantial amount of work being done on Washington Street, but there were also several other matters that needed attention. Jane would be off to the West Side location working until midnight. The next day, the talent (actors) would show up and do what they do, and Jane would be standing-by, and multi-tasking with a focused countenance, and her benevolent way—I'm most certain that the wheels are always turning in this bright woman's head— and making sure that all things were in order in her *Shed*.

Diane Gay

Diane Gay is an artist. She was born in San Diego, California, and studied at Simmons College in Boston; she also studied languages at the University of Mexico. She received a Masters Degree in Industrial Psychology from the Florida Technical University, and went on to work at NASA, where she worked on researching the rate of alcoholism in the Space Program at Cocoa Beach, Florida. She and her husband lived on a sailboat in Daytona Beach, Florida in the early '70s.

In 1978 her marriage ended, and she moved to Westchester County, New York, to live with her elderly mother, whose husband was deceased. It is here, in 1983, that she met her future husband, artist Ray Caram. They met through a mutual friend, and married three years later. Up until that point, Diane's connection with painting was a paint set she received as a gift at the age of twelve.

In the '80s, Ray Caram was a professional artist working in all mediums: oils, pastels, watercolors and drawings. (He was recruited by the Yankees as a pitcher, but didn't care for the life on the road.) He made his living as an illustrator for Ralph Lauren and Avon, as well as other companies. "Ray had limited schooling as an artist, but lots of real life, professional, artistic experience," says Diane. "He offered to teach me to paint. I said no way; I'd been schooled long enough." (Here is where I note that Diane has an independent streak. After seeing some of Ray's paintings of Polo players, I feel sure some other aspiring painter would jump at his offer to be taught by him.) Diane was not an aspiring painter. At that time, she was working with handicapped people, helping them get placement in the work place. However, that would change.

One day Diane and Ray were in an art supplies store, and she saw something which struck her. "I saw these fantastic colors of French dyes painted on silk," she said. Her eyes lit up recalling that memory. As Ray was buying painting materials, Diane bought some bottles of this type of paint and some silk. She went home and read the directions on the back of the bottle, stretched some silk onto a frame, and did her first painting. Diane was now painting, and she was happy with this medium because, "Ray couldn't tell me what to do." Diane had found her *Shed*.

"When I put down a good line and it's bold, I feel good and I want to celebrate," says Diane, regarding how she feels when she's working in her *Shed*. "When I'm painting I'm present for whatever happens," she says. She and her husband were interested in a spiritual discipline called "Advaita Vedanta," which dealt with non-dualism. "Everything is one," she says. I suggest it appears to be similar to a Zen practice, and we discussed removing the ego from the creative process, whether it be painting, acting, or even sporting activities. The writer Rumi is a favorite of hers.

Diane and Ray shared their artistic passions as husband and wife, and painted under the same roof in their home. "We painted every day for twenty years" she said. "We'd have breakfast and then go to different parts of our house." After a day's work, they would look at each other's work, and discuss what they'd painted. They both produced a substantial body of work, and lived off their commissions. Sadly, Ray began to develop symptoms of the cruel disease Alzheimer's, and Diane began the long journey of watching him slip away from their world. His art reflected his decline. "It was as though his painting mirrored what was happening to his brain," says Diane. Ray began painting many bold abstract paintings. (As Diane is explaining this, I happen to glance at a powerful and engaging painting of Ray's; it is the hockey player Bobby Orr.) "He began doing abstracts in which the lines connected, and in time they didn't even touch." This was a painfully obvious benchmark of her husband's progressive disease. Eventually, Ray didn't want to paint at all.

Diane's *Shed* contains her husband's painting table, a blank canvas, works in progress, bookshelves, brushes and other painting accoutrements. I notice also a photograph of Ray holding a baseball bat in his Yankee's uniform, with the City of New York in the background. Diane speaks fondly of her husband's influence on her art. "He encouraged my strong line work." She looks at his table and muses about all of the effort and finished paintings that are part of the table. "It inspires me to have it here; I can't part with it," she says. "Ray gave me confidence, courage and freedom for my work." Diane speaks of Ray's independent and confident spirit.

He gave Diane the confidence to put her work out there commercially. "They'll love it," he told her. "And sometimes they did," acknowledges Diane smiling. "He won a scholarship to the Phoenix School of Design, and was kicked out. Ray didn't like the structure." I'll note here that both of these artists were very independent, and perhaps that is why their "Sheds," could co-exist under one roof. It was a marriage of respect of each other's personality and spirit. "Ray has a unique personality," says Diane, "and he inspired many people."

I notice Diane's painting of a vase of flowers. Its vibrant pinks, yellows and teal flow over the canvas. There's a larger painting of a couple dancing. It's a sensuous image, powerful yet very fluid. The title of the painting is *The Wedding Dance*. The man is in a traditional tuxedo, and the woman is wearing a flowing white dress. Red and orange envelop the couple. Diane uses this painting as her calling card for her work involving the painting of weddings and parties. The more I look at this couple, the more I like the painting. To say Diane's work is sensuous is an understatement. Her work is downright sexy.

There is a copious amount of female energy and power in Diane's work. "I love painting women," she says. People tell her that her work is reminiscent of Matisse, and she was flattered by this. Moreover, she was not really aware of his work; however, the compliment was well-received. As I leaf through photographs of her commissioned and sold work, I see the power, beauty and sexiness of her paintings. In one of her party scenes, I want to be transported into that moment of entwined dancers moving to the strains of cool Jazz. Diane has a calm demeanor; but there is a sensuousness rumbling just below the surface. She showed me some of Ray's paintings of her, fairly large paintings, and they exhibit my aforementioned observation. Ray captured his wife's beauty and power in pastels and oils. His portrayal of Diane is intimate and very feminine.

Diane has produced many works in her *Shed*. She has been a member of the Spring Bull Gallery in Newport since 1998. She is also a member of the Copley Art Society of Boston, where she attained Copley Artist status. Her work has been seen in many galleries in New England. Diane also has paintings in private and corporate collections in the United States, France, England and Holland.

Finally, Diane shares with me Ray's current status. "You need to understand, I lost my best friend." She speaks of, "Staying in the moment, and being open to whatever happens," when she goes to the nursing home where Ray now lives in Newport. She never knows how he'll behave toward her. "Ray teaches me still to stay in the moment, and be present and open to whatever comes my way." This is what he encouraged when they painted and discussed the non-dualism philosophy of Adviata Vedanta. As I'm leaving Diane's *Shed*, I notice a blank canvas, and wonder when the moment will come for her, when she makes her first bold line and wants to celebrate.

Cindy McDonald-Houlihan

The first time I saw Cindy McDonald was 1965, in a church in our hometown. I was an alter boy and was lighting the candles before mass one morning. As I looked out into the growing congregation, I saw a girl sitting in front of Saint Mary, praying. I did a triple take. From that moment, I was praying for a date. We ended up having a ninth grade summer romance, and then moved on to our respective journeys. Four decades later, as the fates would have it we reconnected, and now Cindy and I are man and wife. My wife's *Shed* is the planet earth.

Back Story

As a young child, Cindy dreamed of traveling the world. She read *Hans Brinker and the Silver Skates*, and wanted to skate on a canal in Holland. She consumed literature of far-off places. She read all of Jane Austen's, Bronte's and Dickens' novels, and dreamt of England. As a high school student Cindy did well in school, loved clothing and music; pretty standard stuff. After high school she worked for India Imports, and did some modeling of their clothing line. After having a daughter, and becoming a single mom, she made a courageous decision and moved to London with her daughter Amy in 1971. "I chose England, because I'd read so many British authors."

Cindy was a very shy young woman. "I couldn't walk across a room in front of people, without being petrified," she says. (If you met my wife today, you'd be challenged to believe it). So, she packed up her daughter Amy, boarded a jet and flew to the U. K., "I made that move to get out of my comfort zone," she says. "It forced me to deal with my shyness." This trip to the U. K. was the beginning of Cindy's adventures, which have spanned much of the globe, which is as stated earlier, her *Shed*. Cindy speaks fondly of her time living in Chiswick, a suburb of London, and modeling clothing for a subsidiary of India Imports. She and Amy also lived in a small village in Italy called Allumiere. "People still traveled by donkey in Allumiere at that time." Additionally, Cindy spent time living in the Yucatan in the '70s. "Amy and I lived on the beach in what is now Cancun, before there were any hotels." She and young Amy visited and climbed the Mayan ruins of Chichen Itza. Cindy is a person—like all of the people in this book— who immerses herself in her *Shed*.

As a single mom, Cindy dedicated herself to her daughters— she has an adopted daughter, Tonya—and gave one hundred percent of her energy to motherhood. "My greatest achievements are my children," she says. Like many single parents, she worked tirelessly to provide for her family. Moreover, she cared for her mother during the final stages of her battle with cancer. She also took care of her aging father. It was always about her children for Cindy as a mother, and a caring and dedicated daughter. She cared for and gave unselfishly of herself to the people closest to her.

In 2006, we reconnected through happenstance, and decided to make a life together and get married. Shortly after, her father, then a sprightly eighty-year-old, began a slow and steady decline. He had had fallen from his bicycle and hit his head, which led to a slow paralysis of his entire body. Subsequently, she moved in with her father, and did direct care for him during this cruel and gradual decline. She stayed with her father to the bitter end, and he died in her arms.

After being a witness to my wife's loss and pain through this very difficult time, I encouraged her to reinvigorate her passion for traveling, if that's what she wanted to do. I knew that this was her *Shed*, and that this was the time for her go and be, in her *Shed*. I procured some fun travel tickets for her, and she was off to re-explore her *Shed*. What I didn't realize at the time, was how much, shall I say cultural immersion, Cindy would do for each trip, and how much fun I would have watching her prepare for her travels. I was also very aware of how devastating the loss of her father's was to her, and how these little journeys to her *Shed* was her way of grieving her dad's death. So my wife took this opportunity to go roaming the world.

Paris

Cindy has been to England, Scotland, and Ireland, so she decided her first trip would be to Paris, France. She wanted to stay in Montmartre, and go to the Moulin Rouge, Au Lapinagile (The

Agile Rabbitt), and wander the streets of this "City of Light." I came home from work one day, and heard a haunting female voice singing in French. It was Edith Piaf. On the kitchen table were books of Renoir's and Matisse's work. She'd been re-reading Flaubert's "Madame Bovary," and I also noted a book of short stories by Guy De Maupassant. This would be my wife's modus operandi for her future travels. Cindy was preparing to go to her *Shed*.

When in Paris, she visited the Louvre and saw the "The Mona Lisa." She went to the Moulin Rouge one night, and rode the merry-go-round at the base of Sacre Coeur; she heard the melodic voice of Edith Piaf as she went round and round. She also posed for a photograph in front of the Eiffel Tower, giving the thumbs-up signal— the corny gesture upon my request—and she wandered the streets of Paris. When I picked my wife up at the airport, she was beaming, and looked ten years younger. She literally lit up the airport terminal. Cindy was coming home from her *Shed*, a better version of herself. She was coming back a better woman.

London

A few months went by, and Cindy was looking at a Jane Austen weekend up in Stowe, Vermont. As she was looking at the logistics of going to Stowe, she started checking out some deals in the U.K. to visit Jane Austen's home. She found it was cheaper to go to England then it was to head up to Vermont. I told her to "go for it." She booked the trip that night, and began re-reading several Jane Austen titles. In addition to doing the Jane Austen tour, she took in the stage version of *Billy Elliot*, as well as visiting the Globe Theatre. Again, my wife came home looking happy, energized, and excited for her next adventure. (I told a friend of mine of Cindy's love for traveling, and she said, "The world is her *Shed*"). 'Nuff said.

Mexico City

My wife loves art. Her mother had been accepted to the Rhode Island School of Design, but chose to have a family and forgo an artistic education. "My mother made all of our clothes when we were kids." The way Cindy speaks of her mother's skills using cloth and colors, leads me to see the artistic components of my wife's personality. This creativity was obviously passed on to Cindy. Frida Kahlo and Diego Rivera are favorite painters of hers, so she and a friend who is a painter, decided to head to Mexico City. Stacks of books of Kahlo's paintings filled our home. We watched the movie "Frida." "This will be an art trip," she said. In addition to the museum tours, Cindy climbed the pyramids of the Moon and Sun at Teotihuacan outside of Mexico City, once home to over 200,000 ancients. When I saw the pictures, I was astounded that she actually climbed these things. "I figured while I was there, I may as well climb them," she said nonchalantly. She had a guide accompany her to the top of these ancient Aztec temples. "Climbing up wasn't a problem, but coming down, I needed to hold my guide's hand," she added. "These weren't as big as the ones I climbed in the Yucatan when I was younger, but they were more dangerous." They had to add hand railings to these pyramids because people had fallen in the past, and died. Again, Cindy returned from this trip to her *Shed*, looking ten years younger and happy.

Amsterdam

"After reading *Hans Brinker and the Silver Skates*, I always wanted to skate on a canal in Holland." This is how it starts with Cindy. It could be a painting by Vermeer, or a novel by a Dutch author, and she begins her immersion into that particular culture. Her *Shed*, is one of novelty and adventure. "I always wanted to see the *Girl with the Pearl Earring*, by Vermeer." After reading *Rembrandt's Whore*, and re-reading *Hans Brinker and the Silver Skates*, Cindy started cooking some Dutch recipes. She also booked a puppet play of *Doctor. Faustus* for this trip, as well as a canal boat ride. "I really want to ice skate on a canal," she said. I had no doubt that she would if she could. Needless to say, she wanted to go and see some windmills. "What do you want me to bring you from Amsterdam?" she asked. "A black long sleeved T-shirt," I said. (She'd gotten me a black hoodie that said "Globe Theatre," when she went to London.) As stated earlier, I'm very easily amused. She brought home some great Dutch cookies, and Gouda cheese, and of course my black T-shirt with the words "I *Amsterdam*" written on it in red letters. When I picked my wife up in the airport, from this trip to her *Shed*, she looked tired because she'd decided to stay an extra day. "I feel like I've been gone for a month." When Cindy goes to her *Shed*, she hits the ground running. She's unstoppable.

> **"The day shall not be up soon as I, to try the fair adventure of tomorrow."**
>
> **—William Shakespeare**

One night while Cindy and I'd been eating dinner, I'd mentioned seeing people jumping out of airplanes over in Newport.

"I've been thinking of doing that," Cindy said, looking me with bulging eyes. "In fact Amy did it this week on Oahu with a bunch of people from Maui." Amy now lives on Maui with her husband. I told Cindy if she wanted to jump out of a perfectly good airplane, then she should "go for it." She called the Air Park the next day to book her jump, wanting to celebrate the adventuresome spirit of her father near the anniversary of his death. (Interestingly, Cindy and Amy had not discussed this stuff with each other. Go figure out that one.) So it was off to the Air Park to watch my wife shed the confines of her own "Shed," and jump out of a perfectly good airplane ten thousand feet above Newport and Narragansett Bay. Just another project in her *Shed*.

Costa Rica

A friend of Cindy's said once, "I'd love to go to Costa Rica." Cindy replied, "Well let's go!" (You really need to be careful what you say around my wife). She was on the computer that night booking the reservations for what she was calling, "A nature trip," to her "Shed." Her friend was now caught up in the adventurous swirl of Cindy McDonald-Houlihan, and there was no turning back.

The trip to Costa Rica included dining next to a live volcano and Zip Lining through the jungle. Before this trip, Cindy had injured her forearm, shoulder and pelvis, the result of a bad golf swing (a new tool in her *Shed*.) Nevertheless, she had to go for a Zip Line ride through the jungle. She told me that she had to climb narrow ladders fifty to eighty feet high, to get to the platforms and get harnessed. She also told me that she got stuck on the line, and had to muscle her way to the next platform; this did not help her forearm, pelvis and shoulder. Consequently, she would not be able to go skydiving with Amy, on her next trip to her *Shed*, which would be on to the island of Oahu.

Oahu/Maui

The original plan was to meet up on Oahu with Amy, who would wing over from Maui. Then, the ladies would jump out of a perfectly good airplane—together. Like mother, like daughter. But due to her back injury, the result of the off kilter golf swing, Cindy had to forego skydiving. While on Oahu, she attended the Scottish games. (She wrote her first published piece about the games, for the Saint Andrews Society of Rhode Island). After the games, mom and daughter then flew to Maui, where Cindy took it easy because of her back issue. Normally, trips to Maui would involve horseback riding in the uplands, hiking, swimming and Hula Dancing. (My wife's current status is great, and she is riding her new pink Townie bicycle all around Point Judith, Rhode Island.)

England/Wales

Cindy recently took a trip to the United Kingdom to dance with The Ladies of the Rolling Pin, which is a form of folk dancing in England. The ladies dress in colorful outfits, and do a series of dances, while swinging rolling pins above their heads. The troupe was doing a tour of various parts of England, where they were hosted by other folk dancers. Cindy and her friend were hosted by a couple from Cornwall (which my wife thinks is one of the most beautiful places in her *Shed*). A final side trip was made to a place in Wales called Laugharne. A favorite poet of hers is Dylan Thomas.

It was in Laugharne, on the coast of Wales, that he wrote in his *Shed*, called the "Boathouse." Cindy told me Dylan's wife, Caitlin, would lock him in there at times; the couple had some very serious issues, needless to say. If she heard him talking, she knew he was writing dialogue (many writers say their dialogue out loud when writing), and if he was quiet, she knew he was reading fiction. In Cindy's preparation for her trip to the poet's *Shed*, she'd read a biography by Paul Ferris. In researching Thomas, she found it hard to like the guy.

Upon returning from England and Wales, Cindy bought me a brass miner's lamp for my sailboat/*Shed*. Moreover, she bought us a CD of *Under Milk Wood*, a classic of Dylan's. Listening to this recording made me appreciate this poet's control, and flow of language. (This is elevated text, with scansion similar to Shakespeare's). Dylan Thomas was (in my estimation), a tortured soul, who died in New York City at the age of thirty-nine. When Cindy visited Dylan's home, the caretaker told her he'd never seen anyone linger for so long in the author's "Boathouse." When the man told her that, she told him that she was looking to find something redeemable about this man with a poetic Celtic heartbeat. In the end, she found nothing redeemable about the personal life of the poet Dylan Thomas. At dinner one night, we talked about the power and beauty of Dylan's use of language, and I suggested that perhaps his art is what redeemed him, and she agreed. Cindy McDonald-Houlihan has respect and understanding of other people's *Sheds*. She knows that when a person goes to their *Shed*, they in some way will come back a better version of themselves, a better person.

Shed On!

Currently, Tim Philbrick is designing a new piano casing for Steinway. Mark Holden is playing his drums and reinventing the next great widget. Cameron Greenlee continues to tour the world with the Skattilites, surf, do boat deliveries, and raise awareness of conservation issues on Block Island; Conserfest is ever expanding. Jane Musky is designing a pilot, for a television show called *Smash*. Diane Gay is doing a painting of a sensuous couple waltzing in a mansion setting. Cindy McDonald-Houlihan is planning a trip to Vienna—the land of Wagner and Mozart—to take Power Waltz lessons. Finally, the author will retire to the privacy of his own *Shed*, and continue writing a second novel manuscript entitled, *Dodge Gailbraith's Redemption*.

Nota Bene: Visit the author's "Blogerservations, and informal musings," In his Blog **"Notes from the Docks," on the e-edition of the Block Island Times.**

What or Where is your Shed?

Remember the "responsibility of the question," that I referred to at the beginning of the book. Write well!

Acknowledgements

I would like to thank first and foremost, *The Block Island Times*, especially editor Peter Voskamp, for running the original *Sheds* article. Also, all of the people at the ferry dock in Point Judith, who commented on *Sheds*. Many thanks to Tim, Cameron, Diane, Mark, Cindy and Jane, for letting me come and hang out in their *Sheds*, and see a demonstration of their respective passions. I wish to thank my wife Cindy, who led me to Wharton's, Rockwell's, Melville's and Twain's *Sheds*, that day in the Berkshires, which helped expand this metaphor and make this book happen. I would like to give a very respectful nod to Martin Donovan, and Donny Rooney, my shanty Irish boyos on the job in Point Judith. Also special thanks to former student and aspiring writer Pat Bowlby who continues to teach me. Finally, I say a big thanks to former *Block Island Times'* editor, Pippa Jack, who said that she was, "turning me loose on the world," with my *Blogservations* of the working life on the ferry docks of Point Judith, Rhode Island.

The Author in his Shed on Narragansett Bay